Baby Elephants

Bobbie Kalman

Crabtree Publishing Company

www.crabtreebooks.com

Created by Bobbie Kalman

Dedicated by Samantha Crabtree
To Jada Melia Prantera-Mark,
I love you Boo!

**Author and
Editor-in-Chief**
Bobbie Kalman

Editor
Kathy Middleton

Proofreader
Crystal Sikkens

Photo research
Bobbie Kalman

Production coordinator
Katherine Berti

Design
Bobbie Kalman
Katherine Berti
Samantha Crabtree (cover)

Illustrations
Barbara Bedell: page 8
Katherine Berti: pages 7, 24
Bonna Rouse: page 11

Photographs
iStockphoto: pages 13 (top), 24 (herds)
Shutterstock: cover, pages 1, 3, 4, 5, 6, 7, 8, 9, 10,
    11, 12, 13 (bottom), 14, 15, 16, 17, 18, 19, 20,
    21, 22, 23, 24 (except herds)

Library and Archives Canada Cataloguing in Publication

Kalman, Bobbie, 1947-
    Baby elephants / Bobbie Kalman.

(It's fun to learn about baby animals)
Includes index.
ISBN 978-0-7787-3959-3 (bound).--ISBN 978-0-7787-3978-4 (pbk.)

    1. Elephants--Infancy--Juvenile literature.
I. Title. II. Series: It's fun to learn about baby animals

QL737.P98K34 2010   j599.67'139   C2009-905196-6

Library of Congress Cataloging-in-Publication Data

Kalman, Bobbie.
  Baby elephants / Bobbie Kalman.
      p. cm. -- (It's fun to learn about baby animals)
  Includes index.
    ISBN 978-0-7787-3978-4 (pbk. : alk. paper) -- ISBN 978-0-7787-3959-3
  (reinforced library binding : alk. paper)
  1. Elephants--Juvenile literature. 2. Elephants--Infancy--Juvenile literature.
  I. Title. II. Series.

QL737.P98K355 2010
599.67'139--dc22
                                        2009034830

Crabtree Publishing Company

www.crabtreebooks.com   1-800-387-7650

Printed in China/122009/CT20090915

Published in Canada
Crabtree Publishing
616 Welland Ave.
St. Catharines, Ontario
L2M 5V6

Published in the United States
Crabtree Publishing
350 Fifth Ave.
59th floor
New York, NY 10118

Published in the United Kingdom
Crabtree Publishing
Maritime House
Basin Road North, Hove
BN41 1WR

Published in Australia
Crabtree Publishing
386 Mt. Alexander Rd.
Ascot Vale (Melbourne)
VIC 3032

What is in this book?

What kind of animal?

Elephants are **mammals**. Mammals are animals with hair or fur on their bodies. They are **warm-blooded**. The bodies of warm-blooded animals always stay about the same temperature. It does not matter if they are in the hot sun or in cold water.

Mammals are born

Like other mammals, elephants are **born**. They grow inside their mothers' bodies and come out live.

This elephant calf was just born.
Its body is covered in fuzzy hair.

Mother's milk

Mammal babies drink milk. Mother elephants, or **cows**, make milk inside their bodies to feed their **calves**, or babies. Drinking mother's milk is called **nursing**. These three elephant calves are nursing. They may nurse for two years, or even longer.

The elephant family

Elephants are the biggest land mammals. Elephants belong to the *Elephantidae* family. There are three kinds of elephants. They are Asian elephants, African forest elephants, and African bush elephants. This elephant is an Asian elephant.

Asian elephants are also known as Indian elephants. They have small ears, and very few have **tusks**. Tusks are long pointed teeth. Asian elephants have two bumps on their heads.

African forest elephants have rounded ears, long jaws, and straight tusks.

African bush elephants are also known as savanna elephants. They are the largest elephants. They have huge ears, and their tusks are curved.

An elephant's body

Elephants are **vertebrates**. Vertebrates are animals with **backbones**. Backbones are the bones in the middle of an animal's back. A vertebrate has many other bones inside its body, too. The bones make up a **skeleton**.

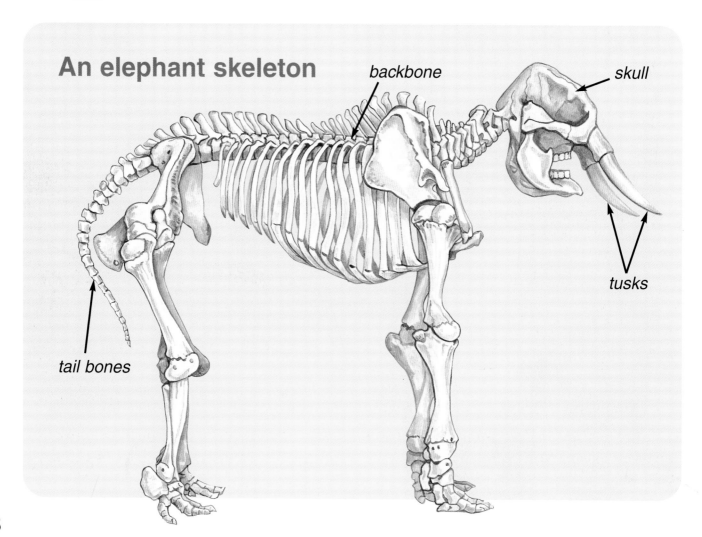

An elephant skeleton

backbone

skull

tusks

tail bones

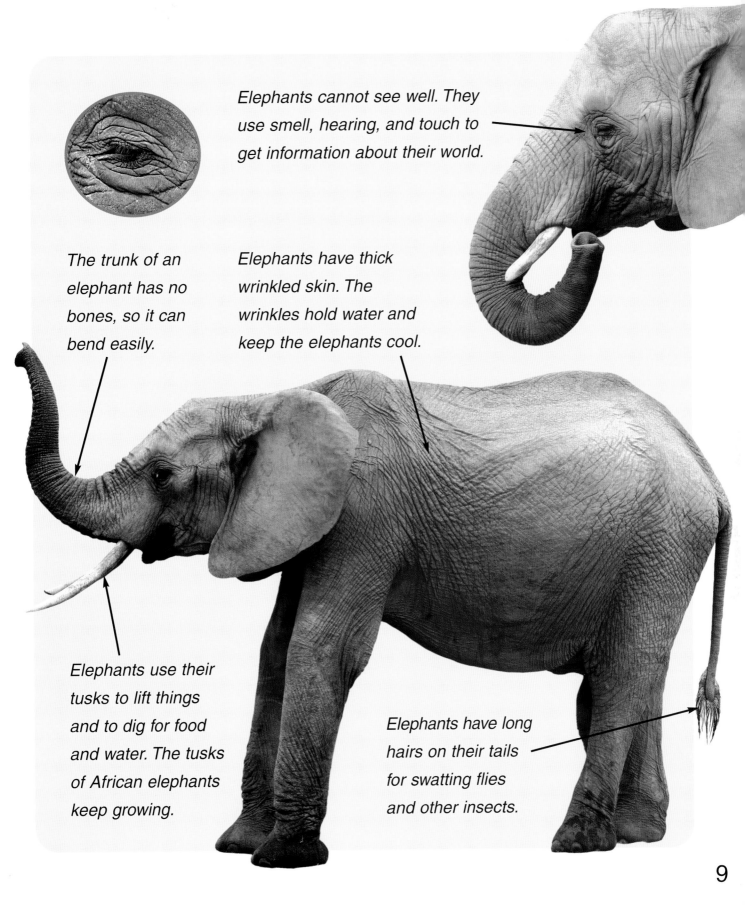

Elephants cannot see well. They use smell, hearing, and touch to get information about their world.

The trunk of an elephant has no bones, so it can bend easily.

Elephants have thick wrinkled skin. The wrinkles hold water and keep the elephants cool.

Elephants use their tusks to lift things and to dig for food and water. The tusks of African elephants keep growing.

Elephants have long hairs on their tails for swatting flies and other insects.

9

Trunks, ears, and feet

An elephant's trunk is its nose and upper lip. Elephants use their trunks to breathe, smell, and lift objects. They are even able to grasp small objects with the "fingers," or tips, of their trunks. Elephants also use their trunks to suck up water and spray it into their mouths or over their bodies.

African elephants have two trunk tips.

Asian elephants have one tip on their trunks.

Elephants can even draw and paint with their trunks!

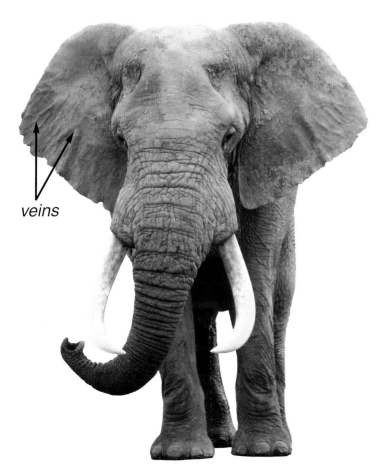

veins

Ears like fans

An elephant cannot sweat, but it can get rid of the heat in its body through its ears. An elephant's ears have many **veins**. Veins carry blood. When an elephant flaps its ears, it is cooling off its blood. The veins let off heat. An elephant's big ears help keep the elephant cool.

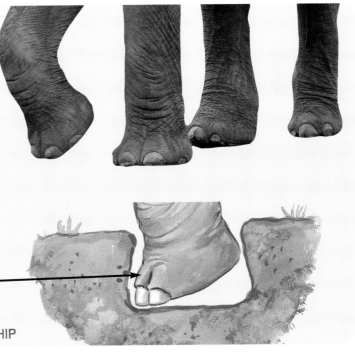

Tiptoe through mud

Elephants walk on their toes. They also have grooves on the bottoms of their feet that grip the ground. The foot of an elephant becomes smaller when it is lifted, to make it easier to pull it out of mud.

Elephant habitats

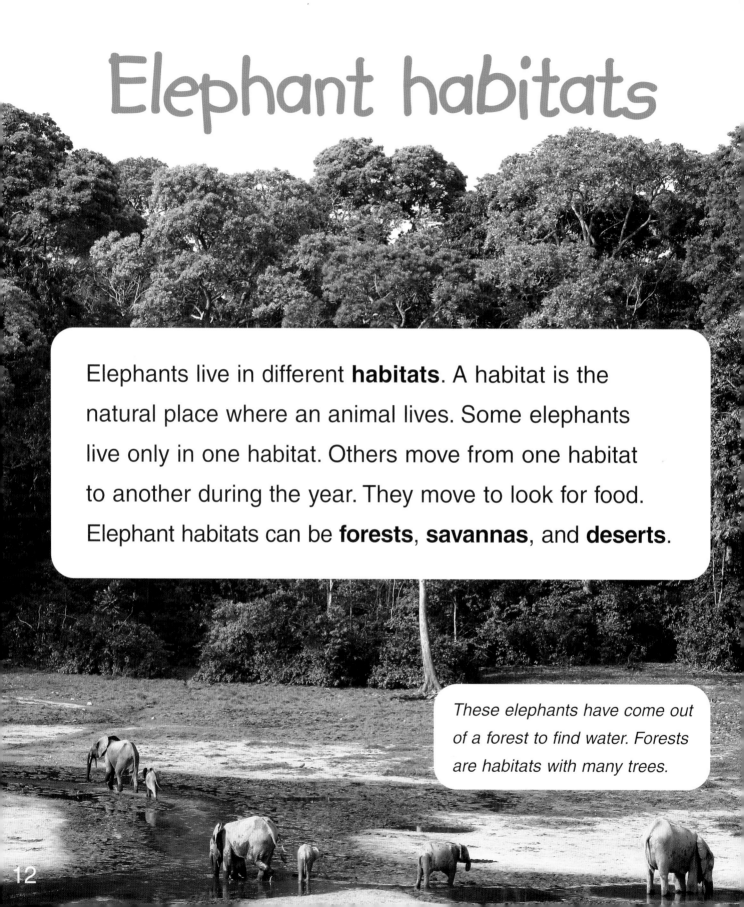

Elephants live in different **habitats**. A habitat is the natural place where an animal lives. Some elephants live only in one habitat. Others move from one habitat to another during the year. They move to look for food. Elephant habitats can be **forests**, **savannas**, and **deserts**.

These elephants have come out of a forest to find water. Forests are habitats with many trees.

These elephants are called savanna elephants because their main habitat is the savanna in Africa. Savannas are large areas where grasses, bushes, and a few trees grow.

Elephants also live in hot deserts. Deserts are dry places that get very little rain. These elephants are running to a water hole to get a drink.

Food and water

Adult elephants eat up to 20 hours a day! They are **herbivores**. Herbivores eat mainly plants. Elephants eat leaves, grasses, roots, tree bark, and fruits such as dates and plums. A baby elephant drinks only its mother's milk for the first four months. Then it starts eating plants, too.

These elephant calves are feeding on grasses and branches. They drink their mothers' milk, too.

Elephants drink a lot of water, but they can go up to three days without it. They suck up the water with their trunks and squirt it down their throats.

Elephants love water! They drink it, bathe in it, and spray themselves to keep cool. They then roll in mud to protect themselves from insect bites. The mud also keeps them cool.

A calf grows

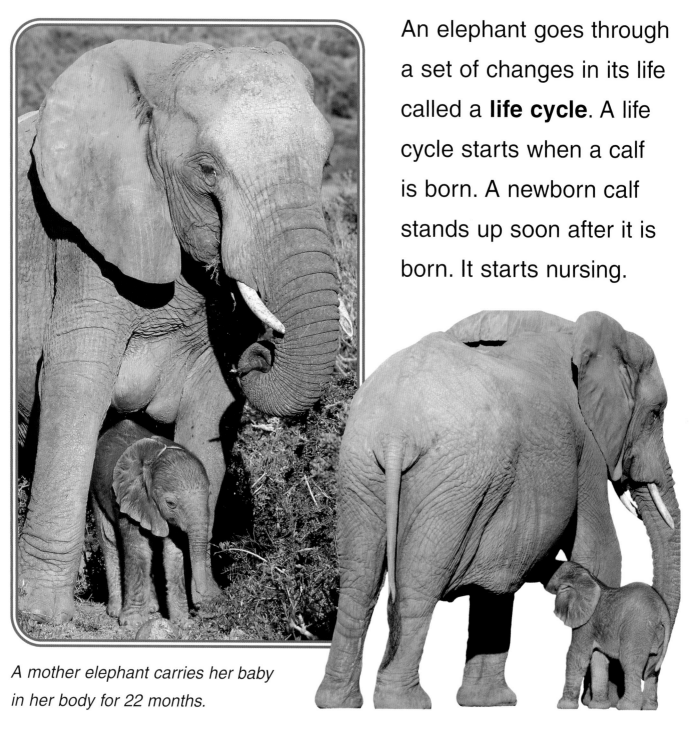

An elephant goes through a set of changes in its life called a **life cycle**. A life cycle starts when a calf is born. A newborn calf stands up soon after it is born. It starts nursing.

A mother elephant carries her baby in her body for 22 months.

The calf grows bigger. It stops nursing and starts eating plants. It is now a **juvenile**. A juvenile is a young elephant. Juvenile elephants, such as these two calves, love to play.

The juvenile becomes an **adult** when it is fully grown. Adult elephants can make babies.

A new life cycle starts with each baby.

Elephant herds

Elephants live in family groups called **herds**. A herd is made up of cows and calves. There are no adult males in a herd. Herds can be as small as two elephants or as big as hundreds. The adult elephants protect the calves from **predators**. Predators are animals that hunt and eat other animals.

*The oldest cow is the head of the herd. She is called the **matriarch**. The matriarch leads the herd to food and water.*

Elephants eat a lot, so they need to keep moving to find food. The members of the herd eat, sleep, bathe, and travel together. They all help take care of the calves.

Some elephant **bulls**, or males, form **bachelor** herds.
Bachelor herds are made up only of male elephants.

19

Elephant messages

Elephants **communicate**, or send messages to one another. They can make about 25 **calls**, or sounds. Each call or cry has a different meaning. Elephants also make low rumbling sounds, called **infrasound**. People cannot hear infrasound, but elephants can hear it two miles (3.2 km) away.

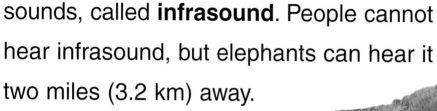
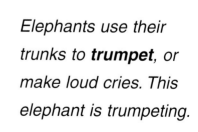

*Elephants use their trunks to **trumpet**, or make loud cries. This elephant is trumpeting.*

Elephants also communicate by showing loving feelings to one another.
This older calf is showing love by hugging a baby elephant with its trunk.

These elephants are saying hello
by wrapping their trunks together.

Elephants in danger

Elephants are **endangered** animals. Endangered animals are in danger of dying out in their natural habitats. Most elephants are losing their habitats. People are building farms and cities on the land where elephants once lived.

This forest has been burned to make more room for farmland.
The elephant calf and its mother may not find enough food to eat.

Many baby elephants lose their mothers when the mothers are killed. People called **poachers** kill elephants so they can sell their **ivory** tusks. Poaching is against the law! Many people still buy things made from ivory, such as this tusk with carvings on it.

ivory
tusk

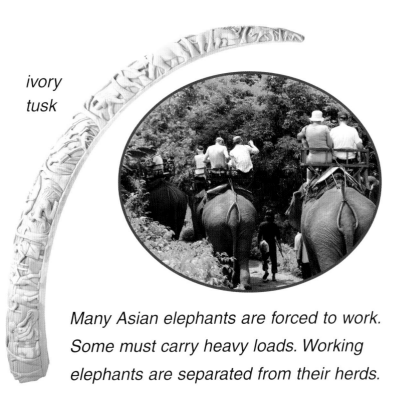

Many Asian elephants are forced to work. Some must carry heavy loads. Working elephants are separated from their herds.

Words to Know and Index

African bush elephants pages 6, 7, 9, 10, 13

African forest elephants pages 6, 7, 9, 10

Asian elephants pages 6, 10, 23

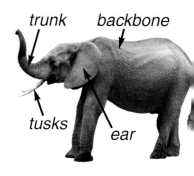

trunk   backbone

tusks   ear

bodies pages 4, 5, 8–9, 10, 11, 16

food pages 9, 12, 14, 18, 19, 22

habitats pages 12–13, 22

herds pages 18–19, 23

Other index words

ears pages 6, 7, 10, 11
endangered page 22
hair pages 4, 9
herbivores page 14
infrasound page 20
ivory page 23
mothers pages 4, 5, 14, 16, 22, 23
predators page 18
tusks pages 6, 7, 8, 9, 23
trunks pages 9, 10, 15, 20, 21
water pages 4, 9, 10, 12, 13, 14, 15, 18

life cycle pages 16–17

messages pages 20–21

nursing pages 5, 16, 17